Ethan's WORD OF HONOR

By Sheri Wall

Art by Given Sharp

A MATTER OF RHYME

Published by A Matter of Rhyme, Killeen, Texas
www.amatterofrhyme.com

Ethan's Word of Honor
Text & Illustration Copyright 2024 A Matter of Rhyme
First Edition

Proudly printed in the United States of America.

Publisher's Cataloging-in-Publication Data
Names: Wall, Sheri, author. | Sharp, Given, illustrator.
Title: Ethan's word of honor / by Sheri Wall; art by Given Sharp.
Description: Killeen, TX: A Matter of Rhyme, 2024. | Summary: Ethan the Eagle is frustrated about his homework. He asks his grandfather to help him understand the word "honor" so he can complete his assignment.
Identifiers: LCCN: 2024918796 | 978-1-958741-07-8 (hardcover) | 978-1-958741-08-5 (paperback) | 978-1-958741-09-2 (ebook)
Subjects: LCSH Honor--Juvenile fiction. | Eagles--Juvenile fiction. | Grandparents--Juvenile fiction. | Conduct of life--Juvenile fiction. | BISAC JUVENILE FICTION / Social Themes / Values & Virtues | JUVENILE FICTION / Family / Multigenerational
Classification: LCC PZ7.1 .W35 Et 2024 | DDC [E]--dc23

A Matter of Rhyme offers discounts when purchasing in larger quantities and offers special educational and promotional pricing.

For more information and classroom activities, please visit www.amatterofrhyme.com.

When Ethan the Eagle came home after school, he complained that Miss Nester had been kind of cruel.

"Now, Grandson, I know that your teacher is fair. Is there more on your mind from today you can share?"

"She gave me a word that I need to explain— by writing a story. It's hurting my brain!"

"What word were you given?" his papa piped in.

"I got the word 'honor.' How should I begin?"

"Honor is quite an exceptional word. It's used as a noun, but it's also a verb.

You should learn a few meanings to get a head start, but true understanding will come from your heart."

"Help me, please, Papa; I want to hear more."

Papa was ready. His joy seemed to soar.

"Ethan, of course, I will share what I know. More knowledge is power. You learn as you grow."

Papa and Ethan went straight to the den
to find some lined paper and also a pen.

"There may be some notes that you'd like to jot down. Let's talk about honor and start with the noun.

"It's honesty,

fairness,

and trust all in one,

and belief in the truth
must be second to none.

" To be given an honor is like an award: a trophy, a pin, or words carved on a board.

"As an honor to others, you've earned their respect, and your work or your life had a lasting effect.

It could be a hero or someone you know, a leader or author who lived long ago.

MR. OWL
AN HONOR TO
OUR CITY

"Are you listening, Grandson?"
He nodded a yes.

"Now, it's the verb that
I'd like to address.

"The action of honor is something you do.
You can honor a promise by seeing it through.

CHORE LIST:
laundry : PAPA ✓
dishes: ETHAN ✓
sweeping: ETHAN

"You can honor your family, your neighbors, your pets,
First Responders, Armed Forces- both current and vets.

Use your good manners. Be kind to each one.
Show you are thankful for all that they've done.

DONATIONS

DONA

FIRST RESPONDERS
TOY DRIVE

"Honor our country; its past will be key.
Learn why we call it the *land of the free*."

Ethan was thinking. He furrowed his brow.
"Honor is making more sense to me now!"

He jumped on his keyboard. His feathers just flew.
He typed up a story from all that he knew.

Ethan kept working, not stopping to rest.

My homework is finished.
I gave it my best.

The papers were graded and getting passed back.
Ethan was nervous but tried not to crack.

He stared at the letter in red at the top, then felt like his insides were going to pop!

The route to get home seemed to take way too long,

yet when Ethan got there, he burst into song!

MEDAL CEREMONY JULY 4TH

Ethan was beaming. He started to glide.

Papa was waiting, his wings spread out wide.

"I'm so very proud. You did well on your task!"
They hugged for a moment until Papa asked,

"Did you make up a story or write one that's true?"

"I wrote one that's true and in honor of you!"

address	to give attention to something
award	a prize given for an achievement
beaming	smiling bright
brow	forehead
burst	to suddenly do something
carved	cut to make a design
complained	said something was wrong
crack	to lose control of emotions
cruel	causing pain or suffering
current	belonging to present time
den	quiet, comfortable room
effect	change that results when something happens

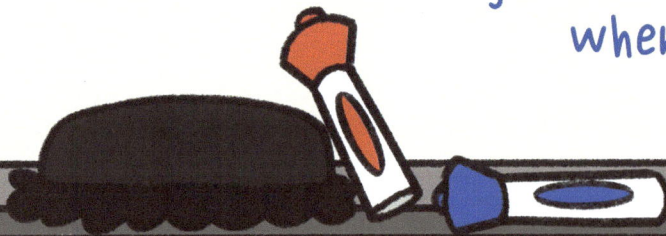

exceptional	unusually good
explain	to make something easy to understand
fairness	quality of treating people equally
furrowed	marked with lines or wrinkles
glide	to move with smooth motion
honesty	quality of being truthful
insides	stomach and nearby body parts
jot	to write quickly
nervous	highly excitable
piped	said suddenly
respect	feeling of deep admiration
route	a way to travel
soar	to increase rapidly
true	real and not made up

Sheri Wall

Sheri Wall is a wife, mom, aunt, grandmother, lifelong Texas resident, and a best-selling children's book author. She established her brand, A Matter of Rhyme, to celebrate rhyming and repetitive verse as fun, essential learning tools. Sheri enjoys cooking, eating, decorating, bargain-hunting, being active, and spending time with her family. See more of Sheri's books at amatterofrhyme.com.

Given Sharp

Given Sharp is an illustrator from Atlanta, Georgia with a passion for children's literature. In addition to illustrating, she assists with youth educational programs at her local botanical gardens. Given is honored to have the opportunity to work on such a special book and would like to dedicate her illustrations to her Papaw, who served in the United States Navy.

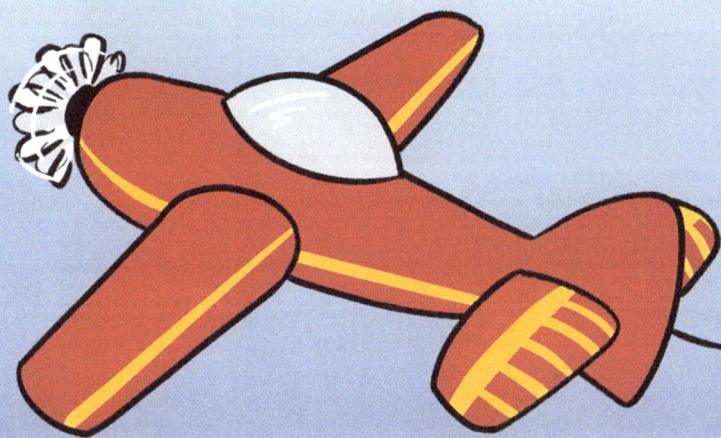

www.ingramcontent.com/pod-product-compliance
Lightning Source LLC
LaVergne TN
LVHW072057070426
835508LV00002B/139